MW00891333

AUSTRALIA AND NEW ZEALAND TRAVEL GUIDE 2023

By James Bartlett

Table of Content

Introduction

Australia and New Zealand are two countries located in the southern hemisphere of the world. They are separated by the Tasman Sea, with Australia to the west and New Zealand to the east. Despite their geographical proximity, these two countries have distinct histories, cultures, and landscapes.

Geography and Climate

Australia is the world's sixth-largest country by land area, covering almost 7.7 million square kilometers. The country is surrounded by the Indian and Pacific Oceans, and it is located between the Equator and the South Pole. Its landscape is diverse, ranging from tropical rainforests in the north to deserts in the central region and temperate forests in the south. The country has a population of over 25 million people, with the majority residing in major cities such as Sydney, Melbourne, and Brisbane.

New Zealand, on the other hand, is a small country consisting of two main islands, the North Island and the South Island, and several smaller islands. It covers an area of around 268,000 square kilometers and has a population of just under five million people. New Zealand is known for its dramatic landscapes, including snow-capped mountains, glaciers, fiords, and pristine beaches.

The climate in Australia and New Zealand varies depending on the region. Australia's northern regions have a tropical climate, with high temperatures and humidity, while the southern regions have a temperate climate with milder temperatures. New Zealand has a maritime climate, with mild temperatures and rainfall throughout the year.

History and Culture

Australia's history can be traced back over 60,000 years when Indigenous Australians first inhabited the land. The country was later colonized by the British in 1788 and became a federation of states in 1901. Today, Australia is a multicultural society, with Indigenous Australians making up around 3% of the population. The country has a strong sporting culture, with cricket, rugby, and Australian rules football being popular sports.

New Zealand's history is also rich in Indigenous culture, with the Maori people having lived on the land for over a thousand years. The country was later colonized by the British in the 19th century and became an independent nation in 1907. New Zealand is known for its relaxed and friendly culture, and its people are often referred to as "Kiwis". The country has a strong outdoor culture, with activities such as hiking, skiing, and water sports being popular.

Getting There and Getting Around

Getting to Australia and New Zealand is relatively easy, with both countries having well-connected airports. Major airlines such as Qantas, Air New Zealand, and Emirates fly to Australia and New Zealand from major cities around the world. There are also many cruise options for those who prefer to travel by sea.

Once in Australia and New Zealand, getting around can be done in a variety of ways. Both countries have extensive public transport systems, including buses, trains, and trams. Taxis and ride-sharing services such as Uber are also widely available. For those who prefer to drive, car rental companies are plentiful, and driving is relatively easy in both countries. However, it's important to note that Australians drive on the left-hand side of the road, while New Zealanders drive on the right.

Australia and New Zealand are two beautiful countries with unique histories, cultures, and landscapes. From the bustling cities of Australia to the rugged wilderness of New Zealand, there is something for everyone in these two countries. Whether you prefer to explore by foot, car, or public transport, both Australia and New Zealand offer a range of options for getting around.

Planning Your Trip

Two of the world's most stunning and diverse nations are Australia and New Zealand. With stunning landscapes, vibrant cities, and unique wildlife, these countries are a must-visit for any traveler. However, planning a trip to these countries can be overwhelming. This guide will provide you with all the information you need to plan a successful trip to Australia and New Zealand.

When to Go

Australia and New Zealand are located in the Southern Hemisphere, so their seasons are opposite to those in the Northern Hemisphere. The best time to visit these countries depends on what you want to see and do.

Australia's summer runs from December to February, and this is the most popular time to visit. The weather is warm and sunny, and there are plenty of outdoor activities to enjoy. However, this is also the peak season, so prices are higher, and popular destinations are more crowded.

If you're looking for fewer crowds and lower prices, consider visiting Australia in the shoulder seasons. The fall (March to May) and spring (September to November) are still great times to visit, with mild weather and fewer tourists.

In New Zealand, the best time to visit is during the summer months of December to February. The weather is nice, and the days are long, making it a great time for outdoor activities. However, this is also the busiest time of year, so be prepared for higher prices and crowds.

If you're looking for a quieter and more affordable trip, consider visiting New Zealand in the shoulder seasons of March to May or September to November. Although fewer tourists are present, the weather is still excellent.

Budgeting and Costs

Australia and New Zealand can be expensive destinations, so it's essential to budget accordingly. The cost of your trip will depend on a variety of factors, including your travel style, the time of year you visit, and the activities you plan to do.

Accommodation is likely to be your biggest expense, particularly in popular tourist destinations. Hostels are a great budget-friendly option, with prices starting at around AUD 20 or NZD per night. If you're looking for something more private, expect to pay around AUD 100 or NZD per night for a mid-range hotel.

Food and drink can also be expensive, particularly in tourist hotspots. Eating out at restaurants can cost upwards of AUD 30 or NZD for a meal, while a coffee or beer will set you back around AUD 5 or NZD. To save money, consider cooking your meals or buying food from supermarkets.

The cost of transportation can vary depending on how you choose to travel. Renting a car can be a cost-effective option, particularly if you're traveling with a group. However, fuel and parking costs can add up, so be sure to factor these into your budget. Public transport is also available in most cities, with prices starting at around AUD 4 or NZD for a single fare.

Visa Requirements

If you're planning a trip to Australia or New Zealand, you may need a visa to enter the country. Visa requirements depend on your nationality and the length of your stay.

For Australia, visitors from certain countries can apply for an Electronic Travel Authority (ETA), which allows for a stay of up to three months. Other visitors may need to apply for a Visitor Visa, which can allow for a stay of up to 12 months. Make sure to check the Australian Government's Department of Home Affairs website for up-to-date visa requirements and application processes.

For New Zealand, visitors from certain countries can enter visa-free for up to three months. Other visitors may need to apply for a Visitor Visa, which can allow for a stay of up to nine months. Make sure to check the New Zealand Government's

Immigration website for up-to-date visa requirements and application processes.

Health and Safety

Australia and New Zealand are generally safe countries to visit, but it's important to take some precautions to ensure a safe and healthy trip.

Health

Before traveling to Australia or New Zealand, make sure you are up-to-date with your routine vaccinations. It's also a good idea to speak with your doctor about any additional vaccines you may need based on your destination and planned activities.

Australia and New Zealand are free of many infectious diseases found in other parts of the world. However, there are some health risks to be aware of, including exposure to the sun, dehydration, and mosquito-borne diseases such as the Ross River virus and dengue fever.

To protect yourself from the sun, wear sunscreen with a high SPF, a hat, and protective clothing. Make sure to stay hydrated by drinking plenty of water, especially if you're spending time outdoors. To avoid mosquito bites, wear insect repellent and cover up with long sleeves and pants.

Safety

Australia and New Zealand are generally safe countries to visit, but it's still important to take some precautions to ensure your safety.

In cities, be aware of your surroundings and avoid walking alone at night, especially in less populated areas. Avoid carrying significant quantities of cash and keep your valuables hidden and protected.

When driving, make sure to follow the road rules and be aware of any hazards on the road. If you plan to hike or explore remote areas, make sure to let someone know your itinerary and bring appropriate gear and supplies.

Finally, be respectful of the local culture and customs. Take the time to learn about the local customs and etiquette before your trip, and be mindful of your behavior to avoid offending.

Planning a trip to Australia and New Zealand can be a daunting task, but with the right preparation, it can be a truly unforgettable experience. Be sure to plan your trip around the best time to visit, budget accordingly, and check the visa requirements before you go. And don't forget to take some basic health and safety precautions to ensure a safe and enjoyable trip. With these tips in mind, you'll be well on your way to an amazing adventure in Australia and New Zealand.

Destinations in Australia

Australia is one of the most beautiful countries in the world, known for its stunning landscapes, diverse wildlife, and unique culture. With its numerous destinations and attractions, it can be overwhelming to decide which places to visit. In this guide, we will explore two destinations in Australia: Sydney and Uluru-Kata Tjuta National Park.

Sydney

Australia's largest and most populated city is Sydney. It is located on the east coast of the country and is known for its iconic landmarks such as the Opera House and the Harbour Bridge. Sydney is a vibrant and multicultural city that offers something for everyone. Some activities you can do in Sydney include the following:

- ❖ Visit the Opera House: The Opera House is one of the most iconic buildings in the world. It is a UNESCO World Heritage Site and hosts some of the most popular cultural events in the country.

- ❖ Climb the Harbour Bridge: The Harbour Bridge is another iconic landmark in Sydney. You can climb to the top of the bridge and enjoy stunning views of the city and the harbor.

- ❖ Explore the beaches: Sydney is known for its beautiful beaches, such as Bondi and Manly. You can enjoy a swim or surf, or just relax on the beach.

❖ Visit the museums and galleries: Sydney has some of the best museums and galleries in the country, such as the Art Gallery of New South Wales and the Australian Museum.

❖ Enjoy the nightlife: Sydney has a vibrant nightlife, with plenty of bars, clubs, and restaurants to choose from.

Brisbane

Brisbane, which is on Australia's east coast, serves as the state capital of Queensland. It is a vibrant and cosmopolitan city that offers a mix of modern and traditional attractions. Here are some of the things you can do in Brisbane:

❖ Visit the South Bank: The South Bank is a cultural precinct that is home to some of the city's best museums, galleries, and theaters. You can also enjoy a swim on the man-made beach or relax in the parklands.

❖ Explore the Brisbane River: The Brisbane River is the lifeblood of the city and is a great place to explore by boat or ferry. You can take a river cruise or hire a kayak and paddle along the river.

❖ Visit the Lone Pine Koala Sanctuary: The Lone Pine Koala Sanctuary is the largest koala sanctuary in the world and is home to over 130 koalas. You can get up close and personal with the koalas and even get a photo taken with one.

❖ Walk the Brisbane City Botanic Gardens: The Brisbane City Botanic Gardens is a beautiful park located in the heart of the city. You can take a stroll through the gardens and admire the various plants and flowers.

❖ Visit the Gallery of Modern Art: The Gallery of Modern Art is one of the largest contemporary art museums in Australia. You can explore the galleries and exhibitions and learn about the latest trends in contemporary art.

Perth

Perth is the capital city of Western Australia and is known for its beautiful beaches, stunning landscapes, and relaxed atmosphere. Here are some of the things you can do in Perth:

❖ Visit Kings Park: Kings Park is one of the largest inner-city parks in the world and offers stunning views of the city skyline. You can take a leisurely stroll through the park or enjoy a picnic with friends and family.

❖ Explore Rottnest Island: Rottnest Island is a beautiful island located off the coast of Perth. You can take a ferry to the island and explore the stunning beaches and natural landscapes.

❖ Visit the Perth Zoo: The Perth Zoo is home to a wide variety of animals, including kangaroos, koalas, and giraffes. You can take a guided tour or enjoy a self-guided walk through the zoo.

❖ Explore Fremantle: Fremantle is a historic port city located south of Perth. You can explore the historic buildings and attractions or enjoy a meal at one of the many cafes and restaurants.

❖ Visit the Swan Valley: The Swan Valley is a wine region located just outside of Perth. You can take a tour of the wineries and sample some of the best wines in Australia.

Adelaide

Adelaide is the capital city of South Australia and is known for its beautiful parks, museums, and cultural attractions. Here are some of the things you can do in Adelaide:

❖ Visit the Adelaide Botanic Garden: The Adelaide Botanic Garden is a beautiful park that is home to a wide variety of plants and flowers. You can take a guided tour or explore the gardens at your own pace.

❖ Explore the Art Gallery of South Australia: The Art Gallery of South Australia is one of the largest art museums in the country. You can explore the various galleries and exhibitions and learn about the history of Australian art.

❖ Visit the Adelaide Central Market: The Adelaide Central Market is a popular food market that is home to over 80 traders selling a wide variety of fresh produce, meats, and cheeses.

❖ Take a tour of the Adelaide Oval: The Adelaide Oval is a historic sports stadium that is home to the Adelaide Crows and Port Adelaide Football Club. The stadium has tours available where you can discover its past.

❖ Visit the Adelaide Zoo: The Adelaide Zoo is home to a wide variety of animals, including pandas, lions, and meerkats. You can take a guided tour or enjoy a self-guided walk through the zoo.

Cairns

Cairns is a tropical city located in the far north of Queensland and is known for its proximity to the Great Barrier Reef. Here are some of the things you can do in Cairns:

❖ Visit the Great Barrier Reef: The Great Barrier Reef is one of the most famous natural attractions in the world. You can take a guided tour or go snorkeling or diving to explore the coral reefs and marine life.

❖ Explore the Daintree Rainforest: The Daintree Rainforest is a UNESCO World Heritage Site and is home to a wide variety of plants and animals. You can take a guided tour or explore the rainforest at your own pace.

❖ Visit Kuranda Village: Kuranda is a quaint village located in the rainforest near Cairns. You can take a scenic train or cable car ride to the village and explore the markets, shops, and galleries.

❖ Take a dip in the Cairns Lagoon: The Cairns Lagoon is a popular swimming spot located in the city center. You can take a dip in the clear, turquoise water or relax on the sandy beach.

❖ Go skydiving: Cairns is known for its beautiful landscapes and views from above are breathtaking. You can take a skydiving tour and experience the rush of jumping out of a plane while admiring the stunning views.

Great Barrier Reef

Off the coast of Queensland, Australia, lies the Great Barrier Reef, the world's biggest coral reef system. Here are some of the things you can do at the Great Barrier Reef:

❖ Go snorkeling or diving: Snorkeling or diving at the Great Barrier Reef is an incredible experience. You can explore the coral reefs and see a wide variety of marine life, including tropical fish, sea turtles, and colorful corals.

❖ Take a scenic flight: A scenic flight over the Great Barrier Reef is a unique way to see the reef from above. You can admire the stunning views and get a different perspective on the reef's size and beauty.

❖ Take a glass-bottom boat tour: A glass-bottom boat tour is a great option for those who want to see the reef without getting wet. You can admire the coral and marine life through the glass bottom while learning about the reef's history and conservation.

❖ Visit a pontoon: Many tour operators offer pontoon tours, where you can spend the day on a floating platform in the middle of the reef. You can go snorkeling or diving, enjoy a meal on the pontoon, and learn about the reef's conservation efforts.

❖ Go on a night dive: Night dives at the Great Barrier Reef are a unique experience. You can see a different side of the reef as nocturnal marine life comes into play, including crustaceans, octopuses, and sharks.

Uluru-Kata Tjuta National Park

Uluru-Kata Tjuta National Park is located in the Northern Territory of Australia and is home to the iconic Uluru rock formation and Kata Tjuta, a group of large red rocks. Here are some of the things you can do in Uluru-Kata Tjuta National Park:

❖ See the sunrise or sunset at Uluru: Watching the sunrise or sunset at Uluru is a must-do experience. The changing colors of the rock formation against the sky are a breathtaking sight.

❖ Walk around the base of Uluru: You can take a leisurely walk around the base of Uluru and learn about the rock's cultural and spiritual significance to the local Anangu people.

❖ Explore Kata Tjuta: Kata Tjuta is a group of large red rocks located near Uluru. You have a choice between going on a guided tour and doing it alone.

❖ Learn about Aboriginal culture: The Anangu people have lived in the area for over 30,000 years and have a rich culture and history. You can take a tour or attend a cultural performance to learn more about their traditions.

❖ Take a camel ride: Camel rides are a unique way to see the landscape and take in the views of Uluru and Kata Tjuta. You can take a guided tour or enjoy a sunset ride.

Tasmania

South of the Australian mainland is the island state of Tasmania. It is known for its rugged wilderness areas, pristine beaches, and charming towns. Here are some of the things you can do in Tasmania:

❖ Visit Cradle Mountain-Lake St. Clair National Park: Cradle Mountain-Lake St. Clair National Park is home to Tasmania's most iconic natural landmark, Cradle Mountain. You can go hiking, mountain biking, or kayaking in the park, and spot unique wildlife such as wombats, wallabies, and Tasmanian devils.

❖ Explore Hobart: Hobart is Tasmania's capital city and has a rich history and culture. You can visit the Museum of Old and New Art, explore the Salamanca Market, or take a tour of the historic Battery Point neighborhood.

❖ Visit the Bay of Fires: The Bay of Fires is a stretch of coastline known for its crystal-clear waters and orange-hued rocks. You can go swimming, snorkeling, or kayaking in the bay, and take in the stunning scenery.

❖ Tour the Tasmanian Whisky Trail: Tasmania has a thriving whisky industry, and you can visit the distilleries on the Tasmanian Whisky Trail. You can sample different types of whisky, learn about the distilling process, and take home a bottle of your favorite.

❖ Visit Freycinet National Park: Freycinet National Park is home to Wineglass Bay, one of the most beautiful beaches in Australia. You can go hiking, fishing, or kayaking in the park, and see unique wildlife such as wallabies and dolphins.

Australia is a large, diversified country with something to offer everyone. From the bustling cities of Sydney and Melbourne to the natural wonders of the Great Barrier Reef, Uluru-Kata Tjuta National Park, and Tasmania, Australia is a must-visit destination for any traveler.

Destinations in New Zealand

New Zealand is a country known for its breathtaking natural beauty, varied landscapes, and extensive cultural history. It offers a plethora of destinations to explore, from bustling cities to serene countryside, from picturesque coastlines to majestic mountains, and lush rainforests to pristine lakes. In this guide, we will explore three of the most popular destinations in New Zealand - Auckland, Queenstown, and Christchurch - as well as some of the stunning national parks that are located within these regions.

Auckland

Auckland is the largest city in New Zealand, located on the North Island. It is a vibrant and cosmopolitan city that boasts a diverse range of attractions, including stunning beaches, world-class museums, bustling markets, and exciting nightlife. The city is also known for its rich Maori culture, and visitors can experience traditional Maori performances, cuisine, and art.

One of the top attractions in Auckland is the Sky Tower, an iconic landmark that offers breathtaking views of the city from its observation deck. Visitors can also take part in a thrilling SkyWalk or SkyJump, where they can walk around the outside of the tower or bungee jump from the top.

Another must-visit attraction in Auckland is the Auckland War Memorial Museum, which houses an extensive collection of Maori and Pacific Island artifacts, as well as exhibits on New Zealand's military history. The museum is located in the beautiful Auckland Domain, a sprawling park that is home to several other attractions, including the Wintergarden, a stunning Victorian-style glasshouse that features exotic plants and flowers.

For those who enjoy outdoor activities, Auckland has plenty to offer. The city is surrounded by stunning beaches, including Mission Bay, Takapuna, and Piha, which are popular for swimming, surfing, and sunbathing. Visitors can also hike to the top of One Tree Hill, an extinct volcano that offers panoramic views of the city or explore the Waitakere Ranges, a beautiful rainforest that is home to waterfalls, hiking trails, and native wildlife.

Queenstown

Queenstown is a picturesque resort town located on the South Island of New Zealand. It is famous for its stunning alpine scenery, world-class ski resorts, and thrilling adventure activities. The town is situated on the shores of Lake Wakatipu, which provides a stunning backdrop for the many attractions and activities on offer.

One of the top attractions in Queenstown is the Skyline Gondola, which takes visitors on a scenic ride to the top of Bob's Peak, where they can enjoy panoramic views of the town and surrounding mountains. At the top, visitors can also take part in a range of activities, including lugging, stargazing, and dining at the Skyline Restaurant.

For adventure seekers, Queenstown is the ultimate destination. Visitors can go bungee jumping, jet boating, white water rafting, paragliding, and more. The town is also home to several world-class ski resorts, including Coronet Peak, The Remarkables, and Cardrona, which offer some of the best skiing and snowboarding in the southern hemisphere.

In addition to its adventure activities, Queenstown also boasts a thriving arts and culture scene. Visitors can explore the town's many art galleries, museums, and theaters, or take a scenic drive to nearby Arrowtown, a charming historic village that is home to several historic buildings and landmarks.

Christchurch

Christchurch is the largest city on the South Island of New Zealand, known for its beautiful parks, gardens, and historic architecture. The city has undergone significant redevelopment in recent years, following a devastating earthquake in 2011, and is now a vibrant and modern destination that offers a range of attractions and activities.

One of the top attractions in Christchurch is the Botanic Gardens, a sprawling park that is home to a diverse range of plant species, including a stunning rose garden, a tropical conservatory, and a native New Zealand garden. Visitors can also take a relaxing punt ride on the tranquil Avon River, which winds through the heart of the city.

Another must-visit attraction in Christchurch is the Canterbury Museum, which houses a fascinating collection of artifacts that showcase the region's natural and cultural history. Highlights include an impressive collection of Maori artifacts, an Antarctic exhibition, and a Victorian street scene that recreates life in Christchurch during the 19th century.

For those who enjoy outdoor activities, Christchurch has plenty to offer. Visitors can take a scenic drive to the nearby Banks Peninsula, a beautiful volcanic landform that is home to several picturesque bays, beaches, and walking trails. They can also visit the Port Hills, a range of hills that provide stunning views of the city and surrounding landscape or hike to the top of Mount Hutt, a popular ski resort that offers panoramic views of the Southern Alps.

National Parks

New Zealand is home to several stunning national parks, each with its unique natural beauty and attractions. The most well-liked ones are listed below:

Fiordland National Park

Located on the southwestern corner of the South Island, Fiordland National Park is one of the largest and most stunning national parks in New Zealand. It is home to several breathtaking natural wonders, including Milford Sound, Doubtful Sound, and the Te Anau Glowworm Caves.

Milford Sound

Milford Sound is a stunning fjord that is known for its towering cliffs, cascading waterfalls, and abundant wildlife. Visitors can take a scenic cruise along the sound, which provides an up-close look at the area's stunning natural beauty.

Abel Tasman National Park

Located on the northern coast of the South Island, Abel Tasman National Park is famous for its golden beaches, crystal-clear waters, and lush rainforests. Visitors can hike along the famous Abel Tasman Coast Track, which winds through the park and provides stunning views of the coastline and surrounding landscape.

Mount Cook National Park

Located in the central part of the South Island, Mount Cook National Park is home to New Zealand's highest mountain,

Aoraki/Mount Cook, as well as several other stunning peaks and glaciers. Visitors can take a scenic flight over the mountains, go hiking on one of the park's many trails, or visit the Sir Edmund Hillary Alpine Centre, which showcases the history and culture of the region.

New Zealand offers a range of diverse and stunning destinations to explore, from vibrant cities to serene national parks. Auckland, Queenstown, and Christchurch are just a few of the many attractions that visitors can experience, each with its unique charm and character. Whether you're looking for adventure, relaxation, or culture, New Zealand has something for everyone.

Accommodation, Wining & Dining

Australia and New Zealand offer a wide range of accommodation options for travelers. The types of accommodation available include hotels, motels, resorts, hostels, camping grounds, and serviced apartments.

Hotels

Hotels in Australia and New Zealand range from budget hotels to luxury hotels. Budget hotels are usually two to three stars and offer basic amenities such as a bed, a bathroom, and a TV. Mid-range hotels are usually three to four stars and offer more amenities such as a restaurant, a swimming pool, and a gym. Luxury hotels are usually five stars and offer the highest level of comfort and service.

Motels

Motels in Australia and New Zealand are usually located along highways and offer basic accommodation for travelers. Motels usually have a bed, a bathroom, and a TV. Some motels also offer a small kitchenette.

Resorts

Resorts in Australia and New Zealand offer a wide range of facilities and activities for travelers. Resorts are usually located in scenic areas such as beaches, mountains, or forests. Resorts offer accommodation in villas or apartments and have a range of amenities such as restaurants, swimming pools, spas, and golf courses.

Camping grounds

Camping grounds in Australia and New Zealand offer accommodation for travelers who want to experience the great outdoors.

Camping grounds offer campsites for tents, caravans, and motorhomes. Camping grounds usually have basic amenities such as toilets, showers, and BBQ facilities.

Serviced apartments

Serviced apartments in Australia and New Zealand offer self-contained accommodations for travelers. Serviced apartments usually have a kitchen, a living area, and one or more bedrooms. Serviced apartments also have a range of amenities such as a swimming pool, a gym, and a laundry.

Dining in Australia and New Zealand

Australia and New Zealand are renowned for their food and wine culture. Both countries offer a wide range of dining options, from casual cafes to fine dining restaurants.

Casual cafes

Casual cafes in Australia and New Zealand offer a relaxed dining experience. Casual cafes usually offer a range of breakfast and lunch options such as sandwiches, salads, and burgers. Casual cafes also offer coffee and tea.

Brunch spots

Brunch spots in Australia and New Zealand offer a range of breakfast and lunch options. Brunch spots usually offer more substantial options such as eggs benedict, pancakes, and French toast. Brunch spots also offer coffee and tea.

Pubs

Pubs in Australia and New Zealand offer a range of pub-style meals such as fish and chips, burgers, and steak. Pubs also offer a range of beers on tap and bottled beers.

Asian cuisine

Australia and New Zealand offer a wide range of Asian cuisine, including Chinese, Japanese, Thai, and Vietnamese. Asian restaurants offer a range of dishes such as sushi, dumplings, curries, and noodles.

Italian cuisine

Italian restaurants in Australia and New Zealand offer a range of pasta, pizza, and other Italian dishes. Italian restaurants also offer a range of wines from Italy and Australia.

Fine dining

Fine dining restaurants in Australia and New Zealand offer a high-end dining experience. Fine dining restaurants usually have a set menu with several courses. Fine dining restaurants also offer a range of wines to accompany the meal.

Seafood

Australia and New Zealand are renowned for their seafood. Seafood restaurants offer a range of fresh seafood such as fish, oysters, and prawns. Seafood restaurants also offer a range of wines to accompany the seafood.

Bars and Wine in Australia and New Zealand

In addition to the diverse dining options, Australia and New Zealand also offer a range of bars and wine experiences for travelers.

Bars

Bars in Australia and New Zealand offer a range of beverages, including beer, wine, spirits, and cocktails. Bars also offer a range of snacks and meals such as burgers, pizzas, and tapas. Bars range from casual neighborhood bars to trendy rooftop bars with stunning views.

Wine regions

Australia and New Zealand have some of the best wine regions in the world, and wine tourism is a popular activity for travelers. Wine regions in Australia include the Barossa Valley, Hunter Valley, Yarra Valley, and Margaret River. Wine regions in New Zealand include Marlborough, Central Otago, and Hawke's Bay. Wine regions offer cellar door tastings, vineyard tours, and a range of accommodation options such as guesthouses and luxury lodges.

Wine bars

Wine bars in Australia and New Zealand offer a range of local and international wines, as well as food to pair with the wines. Wine bars usually have knowledgeable staff who can offer advice on wine selection and food pairing.

Craft beer

Craft beer is becoming increasingly popular in Australia and New Zealand, and there are numerous craft breweries throughout both countries. Craft breweries offer tastings, tours, and a range of beers to try.

Rooftop bars

Rooftop bars are a popular trend in both Australia and New Zealand, offering stunning views of the city or coastline.

Rooftop bars usually offer a range of beverages and small plates to share.

Australia and New Zealand offer a wealth of options for travelers looking for accommodation, dining, bars, and wine experiences. From budget hotels to luxury resorts, casual cafes to fine dining restaurants, and local craft beer to world-renowned wine regions, there is something to suit every taste and budget. Both countries have a vibrant and diverse food and beverage culture, with a range of options available for travelers to experience. Whether you're looking to explore the great outdoors or indulge in a high-end dining experience, Australia and New Zealand have something for everyone.

Activities & Attractions

Australia and New Zealand are two countries that offer a wide range of outdoor activities, cultural attractions, and wildlife encounters. In this guide, we will discuss five of the best activities and attractions in both countries.

Australia

Hiking in the Blue Mountains

The Blue Mountains are located just a short distance from Sydney and offer some of the best hiking in Australia. The Blue Mountains National Park has over 140 kilometers of hiking trails, ranging from easy walks to challenging treks. Visitors can see stunning waterfalls, deep gorges, and unique rock formations. The most popular trail is the Three Sisters Walk, which takes hikers to the famous rock formation of the same name. The Blue Mountains also offer opportunities for rock climbing and abseiling.

Visiting the Sydney Opera House

The Sydney Opera House is one of the most famous landmarks in Australia and a UNESCO World Heritage site. The building offers guided tours where visitors can learn about its history and architecture. The Opera House hosts a wide range of performances, including opera, ballet, and theater. There are also several restaurants and bars inside the Opera House, offering stunning views of the Sydney Harbour.

Surfing in Byron Bay

Byron Bay is a small town located on the eastern coast of Australia and is known for its beautiful beaches and great surf. Several surf schools in Byron Bay offer lessons for beginners and advanced surfers. The town also has a laid-back vibe and is popular with backpackers and travelers looking to relax and enjoy the beach lifestyle.

Visiting the Great Barrier Reef

The Great Barrier Reef is one of the most famous natural wonders in the world and is located off the coast of Queensland, Australia. Visitors can take a boat trip out to the reef and go snorkeling or diving to see the colorful coral and marine life. Several islands on the reef offer resorts and activities such as kayaking and stand-up paddleboarding.

Wildlife encounters at Taronga Zoo

Taronga Zoo is located in Sydney and is home to over 4,000 animals from over 350 species. Visitors can see native Australian wildlife such as kangaroos, koalas, and wallabies, as well as exotic animals from around the world. The zoo offers several animal encounters, including feeding giraffes and petting a koala.

New Zealand

Skiing in Queenstown

Queenstown is located on the South Island of New Zealand and is known for its great skiing and snowboarding. The town is surrounded by several ski resorts, including Coronet Peak and The Remarkables. Visitors can also try other winter activities such as ice skating and snowshoeing.

Visiting the Te Papa Museum

The Te Papa Museum is located in Wellington and is New Zealand's national museum. The museum has several exhibits on New Zealand's history, culture, and natural environment. Visitors can see artifacts from Maori culture, learn about New Zealand's involvement in World War I, and see a giant squid on display.

Wildlife encounters on the Otago Peninsula

The Otago Peninsula is located near Dunedin on the South Island of New Zealand and is home to a wide range of wildlife. Visitors can see penguins, sea lions, and fur seals in their natural habitat. Several tour companies offer guided tours of the peninsula, including boat tours and walking tours.

Hiking in Fiordland National Park

Fiordland National Park is located on the South Island of New Zealand and is home to some of the most stunning natural scenery in the country. Visitors can hike the Milford

Track, one of New Zealand's most famous hiking trails, which takes hikers through valleys, past waterfalls, and over mountain passes. There are also several shorter hikes in the park, including the Routeburn Track and the Kepler Track.

Cultural experiences in Rotorua

Rotorua is a city located on the North Island of New Zealand and is known for its geothermal activity and Maori culture. Visitors can see geysers, hot springs, and mud pools at several geothermal parks in the area, including Te Puia and Wai-O-Tapu. Rotorua is also home to several Maori cultural attractions, including the Tamaki Maori Village, where visitors can experience a traditional Maori hangi feast and cultural performance.

Australia and New Zealand offer a wide range of activities and attractions for visitors to enjoy. From hiking in the Blue

Mountains to skiing in Queenstown, visitors can experience some of the most stunning natural scenery in the world. Cultural attractions such as the Sydney Opera House and the Te Papa Museum provide insight into the history and culture of both countries. And, of course, wildlife encounters such as seeing penguins on the Otago Peninsula or feeding giraffes at Taronga Zoo offer unique experiences that cannot be found elsewhere. No matter what your interests may be, there is something for everyone in Australia and New Zealand.

Practical Information

Australia and New Zealand are two popular travel destinations located in the Southern Hemisphere. While they share similarities, they also have unique characteristics that make them distinct from each other. In this guide, we will cover six practical pieces of information about Australia and New Zealand that can be helpful for anyone planning to visit or live in these countries.

Transportation Options

Both Australia and New Zealand have a variety of transportation options to choose from, depending on your preferences and budget. Here are some common options:

❖ Car rentals: Car rentals are readily available in both countries, and it is a convenient option if you plan to explore the countryside or remote areas. However, driving in Australia and New Zealand can be challenging if you are not used to driving on the left side of the road.

❖ Trains: Both countries have scenic train journeys that are worth experiencing. In Australia, the Ghan and Indian Pacific trains offer luxury travel across the country. In New Zealand, the TranzAlpine and Northern Explorer trains are popular choices for tourists.

❖ Buses: Buses are a popular and affordable way to travel within and between cities in both countries. Companies such as Greyhound and Kiwi Experience offer hop-on, hop-off bus passes for flexible travel.

❖ Flights: Australia and New Zealand have a well-developed domestic airline network, with several airlines such as Qantas, Jetstar, and Air New Zealand offering flights to major cities and regional towns.

Currency and Money Matters

The currency in Australia is the Australian dollar (AUD), while New Zealand uses the New Zealand dollar (NZD). Here are some tips for managing your money in these countries:

❖ Exchange rates: Check the exchange rate before you travel, and consider exchanging money at a bank or currency exchange to get a better rate than at an airport or tourist area.

❖ Credit cards: Credit cards are widely accepted in both countries, but it is always advisable to carry some cash for small purchases and emergencies.

❖ ATM withdrawals: ATMs are available in most towns and cities in Australia and New Zealand. However, some ATMs may charge a fee for foreign card withdrawals, so check with your bank beforehand.

Communication

Australia and New Zealand have good communication infrastructure, with widespread access to the internet and mobile phone coverage. Here are some pointers for keeping in touch:

❖ Internet: Most hotels, cafes, and public places offer free Wi-Fi, and there are also internet cafes in major cities. However, if you plan to travel to remote areas, be aware that internet access may be limited.

❖ Mobile phones: Both countries have good mobile phone coverage, but roaming charges can be expensive. Consider getting a local SIM card or using a travel SIM to avoid high costs.

Etiquette and Customs

Both Australia and New Zealand are known for their friendly and relaxed culture, but it is always good to be aware of local customs and etiquette. Here are some tips:

❖ Greetings: A handshake is the usual form of greeting in both countries, but in more casual situations, a nod or a smile may suffice.

❖ Tipping: Tipping is not expected in either country, but it is appreciated for exceptional service. In restaurants, it is common to round up the bill or leave a small tip.

❖ Dress code: The dress code in Australia and New Zealand is generally casual and relaxed. However, some formal events may require smart-casual attire.

❖ Cultural sensitivity: Both countries have diverse populations, so it is important to be respectful of different cultures and customs. Avoid making assumptions and be open-minded.

Australia and New Zealand are two amazing travel destinations that offer unique experiences and attractions. By understanding the transportation options, managing your money, staying connected, and being aware of local customs and etiquette, you can have a smooth and enjoyable trip. Remember to always research and plan to make the most of your time in these countries. Happy travels!

Travel Tips & Resources

Australia and New Zealand are beautiful and diverse destinations that offer a wide range of experiences for travelers. From stunning beaches to rugged mountains, and bustling cities to quaint towns, there is something for everyone. Here are seven travel tips and resources for visiting Australia and New Zealand:

Packing Advice

When it comes to packing for Australia and New Zealand, it's important to consider the weather and activities you'll be doing. Both countries have diverse climates, so it's important to pack accordingly. Here are some packing tips:

❖ Layers: Bring lightweight layers that can be easily added or removed as the weather changes. A light jacket, raincoat, and scarf are good items to include.

❖ Sun protection: The sun in Australia and New Zealand can be harsh, so pack a wide-brimmed hat, sunglasses, and plenty of sunscreens.

❖ Comfortable shoes: Whether you're exploring cities or hiking in the wilderness, comfortable shoes are a must.

❖ Power adapter: Australia and New Zealand have different electrical outlets than many other countries, so bring a power adapter if needed.

Language Tips

While English is the primary language spoken in Australia and New Zealand, some unique words and phrases might be unfamiliar to travelers. Here are a few tips to help you understand the local lingo:

➜ "G'day": This is a common greeting in Australia that means "hello".

➜ "No worries": Australians often use this phrase to mean "it's okay" or "don't worry about it".

➜ "Kia ora": This is a Maori greeting in New Zealand that means "hello" or "be well".

➜ "Sweet as": Kiwis (New Zealanders) often use this phrase to mean "no problem" or "that's great".

Recommended Travel Resources

There are many travel resources available for planning a trip to Australia and New Zealand. These are a few you should look into:

❖ Tourism Australia and Tourism New Zealand: These official tourism websites provide a wealth of information about attractions, activities, and accommodations.

❖ TripAdvisor: This popular travel review site can help find recommendations on restaurants, hotels, and activities.

Sustainability and Responsible Tourism Tips

Australia and New Zealand are both committed to sustainable and responsible tourism practices. Here are a few tips for travelers who want to minimize their environmental impact:

❖ Choose eco-friendly accommodations: Look for hotels and lodges that have implemented sustainable practices such as energy-efficient lighting and water-saving measures.

❖ Reduce plastic waste: Bring a reusable water bottle and shopping bag to reduce the amount of plastic you use during your trip.

❖ Support local businesses: Eating at local restaurants and buying souvenirs from local artisans supports the local economy and helps to preserve cultural traditions.

Australia and New Zealand are incredible destinations with a lot to offer travelers. By following these travel tips and resources, you can ensure that your trip is enjoyable, responsible, and unforgettable.

Conclusion

Australia and New Zealand are two beautiful countries that offer unique experiences for travelers. From stunning natural landscapes to vibrant cities and rich cultures, there is something for everyone to enjoy. As your travel guide, we have compiled some of the highlights and recommendations to help you make the most of your trip.

Highlights

Natural wonders: Australia and New Zealand are home to some of the most breathtaking natural wonders in the world. From the Great Barrier Reef and Uluru in Australia to Milford Sound and the Franz Josef Glacier in New Zealand, there are endless opportunities to witness the beauty of nature.

Food and wine: Australia and New Zealand offer a diverse range of culinary experiences. From fresh seafood to delicious wines, the food scene in these countries is sure to impress.

Culture and history: Both Australia and New Zealand have rich indigenous cultures and fascinating histories. You can learn about the Maori culture in New Zealand or explore the ancient rock art of the Aboriginal people in Australia.

Outdoor activities: Whether you enjoy hiking, surfing, or skiing, Australia and New Zealand have something for everyone. With a vast array of outdoor activities, you will never be bored.

Vibrant cities: From Sydney and Melbourne in Australia to Auckland and Wellington in

New Zealand, the cities in these countries are vibrant and full of life. You can enjoy shopping, dining, and exploring the local art and culture.

Recommendations

❖ Plan: Australia and New Zealand are large countries, and there is a lot to see and do. To make the most of your trip, it is essential to plan and prioritize the places and experiences you want to have.

❖ Be mindful of the seasons: The seasons in Australia and New Zealand are opposite to those in the Northern Hemisphere, so make sure to pack accordingly. Also, keep in mind that some areas may be inaccessible during certain seasons.

❖ Consider a road trip: One of the best ways to explore Australia and New Zealand is by taking a road trip. You can rent a car or a camper van and explore at your own pace, taking in the stunning scenery along the way.

❖ Respect the culture and environment: When traveling in Australia and New Zealand, it is important to respect the local culture and environment. This includes being mindful of indigenous customs and preserving natural areas.

❖ Try new things: Both Australia and New Zealand offer a wealth of unique experiences, so be sure to step out of your comfort zone and try something new. Whether it's trying kangaroo or bungee jumping, you are sure to make unforgettable memories.

Final Travel Tips and Reminders

❖ Check visa requirements: Depending on your nationality, you may need a visa to enter Australia or New Zealand. Make sure to check the requirements well in advance of your trip.

❖ Get travel insurance: Travel insurance is essential when traveling abroad, as it can provide coverage for medical emergencies, lost luggage, and other unexpected events.

❖ Stay connected: It's always a good idea to have a way to stay connected when traveling abroad. Consider purchasing a local SIM card or renting a portable Wi-Fi device.

❖ Pack wisely: When packing for your trip, make sure to bring appropriate clothing for the season and the activities you plan to do. Don't forget to pack a hat, sunscreen, and insect repellent.

❖ Have fun: Above all, remember to have fun and enjoy your trip to Australia and New Zealand. These countries offer some of the most beautiful and exciting experiences in the world, and you are sure to make memories that will last a lifetime.

❖ Be prepared for the weather: Australia and New Zealand can experience extreme weather conditions, so be prepared for anything. Bring appropriate clothing and gear for hot, cold, wet, and dry weather.

❖ Use public transportation: Public transportation in Australia and New Zealand is efficient and affordable, so consider using buses, trains, and ferries to get around. This can save you money and provide a unique experience.

❖ Respect local customs and laws: It is important to be aware of and respect the local customs and laws when traveling in Australia and New Zealand. This includes things like not smoking in public areas and respecting the sacred sites of indigenous peoples.

❖ Take care of your health: Make sure to stay hydrated, get enough sleep, and practice good hygiene to stay healthy while traveling. Consider getting any necessary vaccinations and bring any prescription medication you need.

❖ Enjoy the local culture: Discovering new cultures is one of the highlights of travel. Embrace the local customs, try the local food, and learn about the history and traditions of the places you visit.

In conclusion, Australia and New Zealand offer a wealth of opportunities for travelers. From natural wonders and vibrant cities to unique cultural experiences and exciting outdoor activities, there is something for everyone to enjoy. By planning, respecting local customs, and embracing the local culture, you can make the most of your trip to these beautiful countries. So pack your bags, get ready for adventure, and have the trip of a lifetime!

AUS/NZ Travel Guide

AUS/NZ Travel Guide

Made in the USA
Thornton, CO
11/11/23 18:05:08

6ded5057-3d7c-413e-95fb-3decc26d6a70R01